Winning the Money Game

Strategies for Successful Wealth Creation

Table of Contents

Chapter 1. Introduction

Welcome to "Winning the Money Game: Strategies for Successful Wealth Creation," an inspiring and empowering Special Report that promises to transform your financial trajectory. This comprehensive guide delves into the crucial tactics and practical strategies required for effective wealth creation, removing the perceived complexity and making it accessible for everyone. The report is filled with easy-to-understand tips, backed by expert insights and real-world examples. Unveil a world where financial freedom is no longer just a dream but an attainable goal. Are you ready to redefine your financial future and take control of your wealth? Dive in and let's win this money game!

Chapter 2. Understanding the Basics of Wealth Creation

Wealth creation stands as the foundation in which all successful financial planning is built upon. It is the process where you enhance your basic financial status to an improved or higher level, leading to long-term financial independence. Understanding the basics of wealth creation is the first step to reaching that desirable stage of consistent money growth and the ultimate financial freedom.

2.1. Elements of Wealth Creation

The process of wealth creation may appear complex, but it is mainly about understanding three things: income, savings and investments. These three elements are the foundation for wealth creation. Let's delve deeper into each of them.

1. **Income**: It is the baseline of your financial picture. This represents how much money you are bringing in, usually on a monthly basis. This income can be from various sources such as your regular job, business, or side hustles.

2. **Savings**: Once you have an income, the next logical step is to save. Consider savings as a buffer for emergencies and a source for your investments.

3. **Investments**: The real journey of wealth creation begins with investments. It is through this you turn the money you've saved into more money. Simply put, you let your money work for you.

The goal is to increase your income, maximize your savings, and smartly invest these savings, leading to the creation of wealth over time.

2.2. Your Financial Goals

Establishing your financial goals serves as the guiding light for your wealth creation journey. These goals can be short-term or long-term, and financial or personal.

For instance, you might have a short-term goal of saving for a vacation or a new car. Alternatively, a long-term goal might be establishing a retirement fund or saving for your child's college tuition. By having these aims in mind, you can create a solid wealth creation plan that aligns with your life objectives.

2.3. The Power of Compound Interest

The concept of compound interest is fundamental to wealth creation. Often referred to as the 'eighth wonder of the world,' compound interest can significantly marvel your wealth creation journey if wisely managed.

Here's how it works: You invest a certain amount of money (the principal), which earns interest. The next time interest is calculated and added, it is done on the initial principal and the interest that was previously added. Therefore, you not only earn interest on your principal but are also paid interest on the interest!

The power of compound interest is noticeably impactful in the long run, making it a potent wealth-creating tool for long-term investors.

2.4. Debt Management

One cornerstone of wealth creation is effectively managing and reducing debt. High-interest debt, like credit card liabilities, directly hampers your ability to save and invest. It's crucial to prioritize paying off high-interest debts while also avoiding unproductive debts that don't wage in your financial favor.

Please note, not all debts are bad. Debts that lead to wealth creation, such as home loans or education loans, can be termed as 'good debts.'

2.5. Creating a Personal Budget

A personalized budget is one of those classic financial tools you can't afford to dismiss. It shows a clear picture of your income, expenses, savings, and allows you to plan your finances for necessary adjustments. A budget keeps you on track, reduces impulsive spending, and ensures your earnings are allocated where you wish them to be - be it investment, savings, or clearing debts.

2.6. Investing Wisely

Wealth creation via investment isn't about quick wealth. Rather, it's a planned strategy where constant, thoughtful decisions directed towards your defined financial goals lead to progressive wealth accumulation. Diversification is key here, for it reduces risk by spreading investments across different assets or asset classes.

Understanding the kind of investor you are (risk-averse or risk-tolerant), and then selecting investment options such as shares, bonds, real estate, and mutual funds accordingly, can ensure you make prudent investment choices. Moreover, it's always a good idea to stay updated about market trends and performance.

2.7. Understanding Taxes

Taxes can significantly scoot your wealth if not managed adroitly. Regular tax planning and utilizing tax deductions and exemptions can result in significant savings, which can be further invested for

wealth creation. Consultation from tax professionals in this regard
might come in handy, providing you with clear tax-saving strategies
that suit your financial profile.

2.8. Embracing Financial Education

Last but certainly not least, educating oneself about financial matters
is invaluable. Understanding financial jargon, staying updated on
market trends, changes in laws and regulations, learning about new
investment opportunities or tax-saving strategies, can be greatly
beneficial. Remember, informed decisions are always more
powerful!

In conclusion, remember, wealth creation isn't an overnight process;
it requires patience, perseverance, and foresight. With a clear
understanding of basic pillars such as savings, investments, debt
management, and budgeting, you're already on the expressway to
successful wealth creation. Embrace your quest to financial freedom,
let the money games begin!

Chapter 3. Setting Your Financial Goals: The Where, Why, and How

In the journey to wealth creation, setting your financial goals serves as your roadmap. It unclutters the route, distinguishing the important milestones from the rough patches, which can lead to the growth of your financial wealth. But how do you set financial goals that not only inspire but also incite action? The answer lies in understanding the Where, Why, and How of setting your financial goals.

3.1. Where to Start: Identifying Your Financial Goals

The starting point in setting up your financial goals is knowing what you desire and envisioning your ideal financial future. The 'Where' speaks to the end game - retirement funds, children's education, owning a home, starting a business, emergency funds, and more. These aspirations serve as your beacon, guiding your decisions and inspiring your actions.

To create a list of financial goals, start by writing down all your desires, both short-term and long-term. Short-term financial goals are those you hope to achieve within a year, for example, clearing a credit card debt or saving up for vacation. On the other hand, long-term financial goals, such as saving for your retirement, span several years or decades.

3.2. Why You Need Financial Goals

Setting financial goals is indispensable, as it provides a sense of direction to your investments and savings decisions. Whether you dream of sailing around the world, launching a non-profit, or underwriting your child's tertiary education, these objectives shape your financial life.

For starters, they serve as a motivating force. Just as a lighthouse directs a ship, goals provide the drive to get up each morning and work toward their attainment. Secondly, financial aims cultivate discipline and facilitate progress tracking. They allow for more informed financial decisions and prevent unnecessary expenses. Lastly, they create the capacity for financial risk-taking. You'll be better prepared to seize opportunities and withstand financial uncertainties that may come your way.

3.3. How to Set Your Financial Goals

To set achievable financial goals, you can apply the SMART goal-setting technique. This acronym stands for Specific, Measurable, Achievable, Relevant, and Time-bound.

1. **Specific**: Your financial goals should be clear, precise, and easy to understand. Rather than setting vague goals like "Save more", aim for more specific ones such as "Save $10,000 for a new car."

2. **Measurable**: You should be able to track your progress. There's a substantial difference between "Increase my income" and "Increase my income by 10% within the year."

3. **Achievable**: Your goals should be realistic, considering your income and expenses. Setting unachievable targets only sets you up for failure and de-motivates.

4. **Relevant**: Goals should align with your vision for your life and your values. Setting goals that you're passionate about increases

your likelihood of achieving them.

5. **Time-bound**: Assign a deadline to each goal. This provides a sense of urgency, which will in turn create momentum for actions.

3.4. Putting it Together: Your Financial Plan

A financial plan is the framework for realizing your financial goals. It includes an analysis of your current financial situation, a strategy for saving and investing, a schedule for your goals and regular reviews of your plan.

1. **Analysis**: Start by understanding your current financial circumstances. Calculate your net worth and analyze your income and expenses. Use this information to get a sense of what's feasible.

2. **Investing and Saving**: Your plan should map out strategies for saving and investing. An emergency fund is a crucial aspect of this plan to cater for unforeseen financial distress.

3. **Scheduling Goals**: Assign feasible timelines to each goal. Long-term ambitions can be broken into short-term attainable targets.

4. **Review**: Remain flexible and adapt your plan as necessary. Ensure to review your financial plan annually or bi-annually.

Remember, setting financial goals and actualizing them require commitment, consistency, and planning. These frameworks can vastly improve your journey towards achieving your targets, leading to a secured financial future, and eventually to financial freedom. With your goals in sight, remember this isn't just about the destination, it's also about the journey - a journey to winning the money game.

With these steps in mind, take time to reflect on your financial trajectory. The power to change your financial life lies in your hands - or rather, in your goals.

Chapter 4. Personal Finance 101: Best Practices for Success

Understanding personal finance is a critical first step to winning the money game and achieving financial success. It all starts with comprehending the basic principles of how to manage, save and invest effectively.

4.1. Understanding the Basics

To lay the proper groundwork for financial success, it's first necessary to familiarize yourself with the basic terminologies in personal finance. These terms apply universally, regardless of your financial situation:

- **Income:** Money that an individual or business receives in exchange for providing a good or service or through investing capital. It can be in the form of wages from your job, rental income, or profits from investments.

- **Expenses:** Money spent on goods or services. These can include fixed expenses, such as rent or mortgage, car payments, and insurance premiums, as well as variable expenses such as groceries, entertainment, and vacations.

- **Savings:** Money set aside for future use. Ideally, savings should amount to at least 20% of your income and be utilized for retirement, emergencies, and major purchases.

- **Investments:** Assets or items acquired with the goal of generating income or appreciation in value. Investments can range from physical assets like real estate or gold to financial assets like stocks, bonds, or mutual funds.

4.2. Develop a Budget

The next step towards mastering personal finance is to develop a budget that gives you a clear overview of your income and expenses. An essential part of budgeting includes the 50/30/20 rule. It suggests that 50% of your income should go towards necessities, 30% towards discretionary items, and 20% should be saved or invested.

4.2.1. Creating Your Budget

The following steps can help create a basic, but effective budget:

1. Write down your total income: Quantify your total income on an after-tax basis. This includes salary, financial assistance, dividends, or any other type of income you receive.

2. Track your expenses: Now list out all your fixed and variable expenses. Ensure you are honest and accurate about the amounts to avoid misleading results.

3. Categorize your expenses: Differentiate between your spending into three categories - needs, wants, and savings or debt repayments. This aligns with the 50/30/20 rule, helping you balance your financial needs and wants with your financial goals.

4. Adjust your spending or increase income: If you are unable to save or invest 20% of your income, consider finding ways to minimize expenses or increase income.

Once the budget is established, you must continuously monitor it and adjust as needed. Over time, you'll gain more control over your finances and will be better prepared to adjust to changes in income or unexpected expenses.

4.3. Saving Wisely

Saving is fundamental for building wealth. Not only does it provide a safety net for unforeseen costs, but it also allows for investments, accumulating greater wealth.

4.3.1. Building an Emergency Fund

The first step in saving is to create an emergency fund which ideally holds three to six months' worth of living expenses. This fund should readily be accessed during a sudden job loss, medical emergencies, or unexpected large expenses.

4.3.2. Setting Financial Goals

Next, save towards specific financial goals. These could be short-term, like journeys or tech gadgets, medium-term goals such education expenses, or long-term goals like retirement.

4.4. Understanding and Managing Debt

Debt is often a necessary part of personal finance, but it's also one that can take away financial freedom if not managed properly.

It is important to understand 'good debt' and 'bad debt'. Good debt typically comes with low interest rates and improves your financial position in the long run (e.g., education loans, mortgage). Bad debt, on the other hand, can quickly accrue high interest and provides little to no long-term benefit (e.g., credit cards, personal loans).

Managing debt requires paying off bad debts as soon as possible and making regular, timely payments for good debts.

4.5. Investing for the Future

The last piece of the personal finance puzzle is investing. Investing allows your money to grow, helping you to reach your financial goals more quickly.

Understand the different types of investments - stocks, bonds, mutual funds, and real estate, among others - and how they can serve you. Each type of investment has different levels of risk and return associated with it. Balance your portfolio with a mix of investments in different sectors to mitigate risk.

In conclusion, mastering your personal finances isn't as difficult as it first appears. By understanding the basics, creating and sticking to a budget, saving wisely, handling debt, and investing for the future, you are setting up a solid foundation for financial freedom. It's simply about taking control and making decisions that guide you towards your financial goals. The better you get at these tactics, the closer you become to winning the money game.

Chapter 5. Investing: The Key Towards Accumulating Wealth

Wealth creation is an accumulation process that requires patience, discipline, and a complete understanding of different investment options. Investing, in financial terms, refers to allocating your money in different financial instruments with the expectation of earning an optimal return over time. But do not confuse investing with saving, as the latter preserves your capital, while the former grows it.

5.1. Understanding the Basics of Investing

First and foremost, it's important to understand the basic concepts associated with investing. We'll explore a few key terms:

Principal: This is the original sum of money you invest.

Return: This is the money you earn from your investment, it can be in the form of income (like interest or dividends) or capital gain (an increase in the value of your investment).

Risk: There's potential for your investment value to rise or fall. Different investments have different levels of risk.

Diversification: Spreading your investments across a variety of assets to reduce risk. The theory here is that if one investment performs poorly, others might perform well.

Compound Interest: Earnings on your investment get reinvested, and they also start earning, thereby compounding your returns over time.

Investors should strive to gain a thorough understanding of the basic principles of investing before moving forward with specific investment strategies.

5.2. Asset Allocation and Diversification

Investing is not just about what investments you choose, but also how you divide your investments. This is called asset allocation. At its simplest, asset allocation is about balancing risk and reward by dividing a portfolio's assets according to an individual's financial goals, risk tolerance, and investment horizon.

Diversification, a key component of asset allocation strategy, is also an important concept in investing. By spreading investments across various types of financial instruments, sectors, and other categories, investment risk can be managed more effectively. No single investment dominates the entire portfolio, hence, any potential loss from one investment can be offset by gains from another.

5.3. The Power of Compound Interest

The concept of compound interest is one of the major pillars for effective wealth creation through investing. Compounding can be defined as earning returns on the returns. In other words, when the returns from an investment are reinvested and start earning returns themselves, this phenomenal financial formula begins to snowball and can greatly enhance your wealth over time.

5.4. Types of Investments

There are various vehicles you can use for investing, and we'll take a look at several of the most common ones:

Stocks: When you invest in a company's stock or shares, you own a piece of that company. Stocks have the potential for high returns but also carry high risk.

Bonds: These are like loans to a company or the government. Bondholders earn periodic interest payments and get back their invested money after a certain period.

Mutual Funds: These are investment vehicles managed by professionals. They pool money from numerous investors and invest it in different assets, providing diversification.

Real Estate: Real estate investing might involve buying properties for rental income, or buying and selling properties for profit.

Exchange-Traded Funds (ETFs): These are similar to mutual funds but are traded on stock exchanges. ETFs can give exposure to a wide range of assets.

Cryptocurrencies: Digital or virtual currencies that use cryptography for security. Cryptocurrencies like Bitcoin and Ethereum are high-risk, high-reward investments.

5.5. Choosing an Investment Strategy

Choosing the right investment strategy plays a critical role in wealth accumulation. Here are some strategies you might consider:

Value Investing: This strategy involves buying stocks that appear to be undervalued in the market. The mantra here is to buy low and sell high.

Income Investing: This strategy focuses on building a portfolio that generates a regular and steady income stream. This usually involves investing in bonds or dividend-paying stocks.

Growth Investing: This strategy involves investing in companies that exhibit signs of above-average growth, even if the share price appears expensive in terms of metrics like Price/Earnings ratios.

Small-Cap Investing: This strategy involves investing in smaller companies that have a market cap of under $1 billion. The theory is these small companies have more room for growth compared to larger, more established companies.

Socially Responsible Investing (SRI): This strategy involves investing in companies that align with the investor's personal values. For instance, an SRI investor might choose companies that are known for their environmental stewardship, social justice efforts, or ethical business practices.

Remember, your investment strategy should be aligned with your financial goals, risk profile, and investment horizon. An understanding of the investment landscape, awareness about financial markets, and patience are prerequisites to winning the investment game.

The journey of investing and wealth accumulation does not stop here. Continuous learning and staying informed about market trends should be an integral part of your investment journey. Now that you're equipped with the fundamentals of investing, let the journey of creating wealth begin.

Chapter 6. Navigating the Stock Market: Understanding Risks and Rewards

Investing in the stock market is a prominent vehicle for wealth creation, offering the potential for high returns over the long term. Yet, it is not without its challenges and risks. Without a firm grasp of how the stock market operates, one can quickly get lost or even worse, make expensive errors. This chapter equips you with the fundamental understanding and practical applications necessary to navigate the stock market, shining light on both the rewards and risks involved.

===Understanding the Stock Market

The stock market is not a single entity but rather a network of exchanges where publicly traded companies list their shares. Some well-known stock exchanges include the New York Stock Exchange (NYSE), NASDAQ, and the London Stock Exchange (LSE). Stocks or shares represent ownership in a company and holders of these shares, termed as shareholders, have an equity stake in that company. They can profit from these shares in two primary ways: through any dividend payments the company issues and through capital appreciation if they sell their shares at a higher price than what they initially paid.

But why do companies issue shares? Companies issue shares to raise capital. They do this during an event called an Initial Public Offering (IPO), which marks a company's transition from private to public. Once publicly traded, a company's shares are traded between investors on the secondary market – the stock market we are familiar with.

===Risk and Reward in the Stock Market

Investing in the stock market involves risk, but its potential returns make it one of the most popular investment strategies. Common types of risks associated with stock market investing are income risk, capital risk, and market risk. Income risk pertains to the possibility of the company cutting dividends, which can subsequently lead to decreasing stock prices. Capital risk covers the possibility of losing all the capital invested if a company goes bankrupt. Market risk is the potential loss due to factors that affect the overall performance of the financial market.

On the upside, the stock market offers potentially high returns, both through capital appreciation and dividend payments. Stocks historically have a higher rate of return than other investment types on average.

===Essential Principles for Navigating the Stock Market

- Process Over Outcome: Successful stock market investors focus more on building sound investment processes rather than obsessing over short-term outcomes. They understand market trends, evaluate investment options critically, and make data-driven decisions.

- Diversification: This is a practical way to manage risk. Instead of investing in one stock, smart investors spread their investments across various sectors, industries, and geographic regions to lower risk.

- Understand What You Own: Due diligence and thorough research before buying stocks is a crucial investment principle. The more you understand the company, its industry, and its potential growth drivers, the better you can evaluate its future prospects.

- Stay Consistent: The stock market's nature can test investor patience. Amid short-term volatility, investors who stay disciplined and stick to their strategy typically see more substantial long-term gains.

=== Basic Stock Market Investing Strategies

Different investors adopt different strategies based on their priorities, risk tolerance, and time horizon. Yet, some commonly adopted strategies are:

- Buy and Hold: This long-term investment strategy involves buying stocks and holding onto them for a prolonged period. It is based on the belief that over time, the stock market will deliver a decent return despite periods of decline or stagnation.

- Value Investing: This strategy involves identifying and buying shares of companies that appear to trade for less than their intrinsic or book value. Value investors actively seek stocks they believe the market has undervalued.

- Growth Investing: Growth investors invest in high-growth companies. These stocks are often more expensive, but growth investors believe the company's rapid growth will justify the premium price over time.

It's not just about "investing money" or "buying low and selling high." Navigating the stock market is about understanding companies, gauging market sentiment, calculating risks, and aligning these elements with your financial goals. With informed decisions, a disciplined approach, and resilience, you can use the stock market as a powerful tool for wealth creation. This chapter sought to equip you with a solid foundation to help you on this journey; the rest is up to you.

Chapter 7. Real Estate Investments: Let the Buildings Speak Money

Real estate investment, contrary to popular belief, is not solely about buying a property and then renting or selling it. It's fundamentally a business proposition, which involves assessing financial viability, potential returns, and risks before making a decision. Grounded in this understanding, this chapter delves into the complex alleys of real estate investment.

7.1. Understanding the Real Estate Business Cycle

The business cycle of real estate is marked by four primary stages – Recovery, Expansion, Hyper Supply, and Recession. A wise investor is one who understands these stages and makes investments aligned with these cycles.

The Recovery phase is marked by low demand, but it is here that you can bag potentially high-return deals. Next is the Expansion phase, where demand increases, and new constructions start emerging. The Hyper Supply is when construction exceeds the market demand. When investing during this phase, caution must be employed as the supply-demand balance is drastically tilted. Finally, the Recession phase arrives, characterized by a considerably lower demand than supply, leading to a drop in prices.

Learning how to decipher these cycles necessitates a comprehensive understanding of the overall economy, local market conditions, and property-specific factors. This knowledge empowers you to take calculated risks, potentially reaping substantial returns.

7.2. Identifying Profitable Investment Properties

Identifying profitable investment properties requires you to analyze variables like location, market trends, and property condition. Locations with growing job markets, developing infrastructure, and good schools tend to have higher rental rates, subsequently attracting quality tenants.

Understanding property-specific characteristics such as the condition of the property, renovation costs, and potential capital gains are paramount. Engaging a professional building inspector is a prudent move, to avoid hidden renovation costs that can lower your returns.

7.3. Financing Your Real Estate Investment

Financing your real estate investment accurately is vital as erroneous decisions could lead to a financial debacle. Some primary ways to finance your investment are through home equity loans, real estate partnerships, hard money lenders, or investment property loans. The optimum financing strategy could vary based on the risk associated with the property, economic conditions, and your credit score.

A common mistake committed by many novice investors is over-leveraging. While loans can help you diversify your investment portfolio, recklessly borrowing can lead to a debt trap.

7.4. The Power of Passive Income

One of the most appealing aspects of real estate investing is the generation of passive income. Rental properties, for instance, provide a steady cash flow if managed well. Invest time in understanding rental yields, vacancy rates, and tenant retention strategies to maximize this income stream.

Investing in Real Estate Investment Trusts (REITs) is another option. REITs are companies owning income-generating real estate, and investing in them allows you to enjoy real estate returns without owning physical properties.

7.5. Risks in Real Estate Investment

While real estate presents lucrative opportunities, navigating the investment landscape without understanding the risks can be perilous. Key risks include property market fluctuations, interest rate changes, unexpected renovation costs, vacancies, and undesirable tenants.

Proactive risk management steps, like disciplined financial planning, property insurance, diligent tenant screening, and preventive maintenance, can mitigate these risks to a large extent.

7.6. Building a Real Estate Portfolio

Building a successful real estate portfolio involves diversification, constant learning, regularly monitoring your investments, and adaptability. Diversification minimizes risk - you can invest in residential, commercial, and rental properties located in different geographical regions. Regular portfolio review helps you assess whether your investments align with your financial goals.

Whether you plan to invest in residential properties, commercial properties, rent out a vacation home, or delve into the world of REITs, successful real estate investment requires a combination of comprehensive knowledge, discipline, clear goals, and risk-taking ability. Done right, it can significantly contribute to your overall wealth creation, making your money work, or in this case, making your buildings speak money.

Chapter 8. Retirement Planning: The Golden Years of Freedom

The journey towards retirement can often seem a daunting one - packed with decisions to make, investments to consider, and monetary goals to achieve. Yet, the promise of the golden years of freedom lies within the grasp of anyone willing to embark on intentional, thoughtful retirement planning.

8.1. Introduction to Retirement Planning

Understanding your financial needs for your retirement years is the building stone of successful wealth creation. Retirement planning involves calculating your projected expenses, managing risk, and creating a feasible savings and investment plan to ensure your financial security in the later years of your life.

8.2. Assessing Your Retirement Needs

To begin with, you need to realistically assess how much income you will require in retirement based on your projected lifestyle, life expectancy, potential healthcare costs, and other necessary expenses such as housing, transport, and everyday living costs. We live in a world where longevity is increasing, and with it, the potential cost of retirement. Moreover, keep in mind inflation and the fact that the cost of living is likely to be much higher in the future.

8.3. Establishing a Savings Plan

Once you've determined your retirement income needs, the next step is to develop a disciplined savings plan. The earlier you start, the longer your money will have time to grow due to the magic of compounding. You could automate your savings by setting aside a certain percentage of your income each month into your retirement account.

8.4. Diversifying Your Investments

Financial experts often highlight the importance of diversifying your investments. Having a mix of assets, such as stocks, bonds, and real estate, may help mitigate the risk while potentially amplifying your overall returns. It's wise to revise your asset allocation as you get closer to retirement, typically shifting towards more conservative investments to safeguard your accumulated wealth.

8.5. Making the Most of Employee Benefits

Several employers offer retirement benefits like 401(k), 403(b), and other pension plans, often matching a percentage of the employee's contribution. It's crucial to take full advantage of such benefits not just for the savings, but also for the tax advantages they potentially offer.

8.6. Understanding Social Security Benefits

Understanding when and how to claim Social Security benefits can significantly impact your overall retirement income. Remember that these benefits increase with the age at which you start claiming them, with the maximum benefit available if you delay until the age of 70.

8.7. Planning for Healthcare Expenses

With age, healthcare expenses tend to rise. Planning for these costs is a pivotal part of retirement planning. Look for ways to cover such expenses, be it through Medicare, Medigap, or long-term care insurance.

8.8. Estate Planning

Estate planning, including wills, trusts, and power of attorney, should be an integral part of your retirement planning. It ensures your assets are distributed according to your wishes after your death and can help reduce tax burdens on your estate.

8.9. Retirement and Taxation

Understanding tax implications on your retirement income sources is crucial. This may include taxes on Social Security benefits, retirement account withdrawals, and investment income. Working with a tax advisor or a financial planner can ensure you strategize not only for wealth creation but also for its preservation post-retirement.

Retirement planning is an ongoing process, and an early start can yield significant benefits. A financially secure retirement doesn't happen by mere chance. It's the direct result of a well-structured plan, disciplined saving, and prudent investment. Securing your golden years of freedom relies heavily upon making informed decisions today. Allow this comprehensive guide to illuminate your path as you navigate the journey towards a rewarding retirement.

The freedom to enjoy your time, pursue your passions, and leave a legacy is possible. So, gear up, strategize your game, and let's bask in the victory that awaits in your retirement years.

Chapter 9. Tax Planning: Smart Strategies to Maximize Savings

The journey on the road to wealth creation often includes bumpers and barriers, but one of the most significant and yet, most overlooked is tax planning. This is a crucial aspect of managing your finances, often determining the difference between wealth creation and wealth erosion. Efficient tax planning, when done correctly, can provide you with the money needed to invest in your future.

9.1. Understanding Taxes

To maximize your savings, you first need to understand how taxes work – particularly those that apply to your income, investments, and estate. Let's start with income tax. This is the money deducted from your paycheck each week, month, or year, depending on your employer's payment schedule. How much you're taxed depends heavily on your "tax bracket" which is a range of incomes taxed at a given rate.

Investment taxes are assessed on any profits you make on your investments, including stocks, bonds, mutual funds, and real estate. The rate at which these gains are taxed often depends on how long you held the investment before selling it.

Estate tax, although not applicable to everyone, is a tax levied on the total value of a person's estate (property, money, and possessions) at the time of their death. For the majority of individuals, estate tax liabilities can be eliminated or significantly reduced through proper tax planning.

Knowing these basics helps us identify potential areas where we can maximize savings. The key here is always to be proactive and think ahead.

9.2. Income Shifting Strategies

A prominent strategy for tax planning revolves around shifting income to different periods or persons to take advantage of lower tax rates. Here are a few methods you can use:

1. Use of Retirement Accounts: If your employer offers a retirement account like a 401(k) or traditional IRA, maximize your contributions. The money you put in these accounts isn't taxed until you withdraw it in retirement (when you'll likely be in a lower tax bracket).

2. Transferring Income to Family Members: If you have a high tax bracket, you might consider shifting income to family members in lower tax brackets. This can be done through gifting assets or earnings.

3. Deferring Income: If you think you'll retire or otherwise have a lower income within a few years, you might consider deferring bonuses, or additional income, into those years when your tax bracket will be lower.

9.3. Investment-Specific Tax Tactics

Not all investments are created equal in the eyes of the taxman, and the way you manage your portfolio can make a significant impact on your savings. Here are a few essential tips:

1. Tax-Efficient Investing: Investments have different tax rates. Long-term investments (held for more than one year) tend to be taxed at a lower rate than short-term investments. It might be strategic to hold onto certain investments longer to take advantage of these rates.

2. Tax-Sheltered Accounts: Certain types of accounts, like IRAs and 401(k)s, are 'tax-sheltered', meaning the investments inside them grow tax-deferred or tax-free. Try to maximize your contributions to these accounts.

3. Strategic Selling: Sell investments at strategic times to offset capital gains through capital losses. This strategy, known as "tax-loss harvesting," can significantly reduce your tax bill.

9.4. Estate Tax Planning

While the majority may not face estate taxes, it's still crucial to establish a plan for your estate's succession, to ensure your hard-earned wealth is transferred according to your wishes, and to minimize any potential taxes. Consider the following strategies:

1. Gifting: Giving some of your estate to heirs each year may help to gradually reduce the size of your estate and the associated tax.

2. Trusts: These are legal arrangements that can serve to protect assets, reduce estate taxes, avoid probate, and manage assets for beneficiaries.

3. Life Insurance: The death benefit of life insurance is typically exempt from income taxes for the beneficiaries. Moreover, with the right structuring, it can also be exempt from estate tax.

9.5. Tax Laws and Deductions

Never underestimate the importance of staying up-to-date on the current tax laws and potential deductions. Regulations change often, and what might not have been an attractive strategy previously could now be beneficial. Make use of various deductions and tax credits, especially those aligned with environmentally-friendly choices and health-related expenses.

In conclusion, tax planning should not be an afterthought but an integral part of your wealth creation journey. Partner with a savvy tax advisor and implement these strategies to boost your savings and optimize your wealth creation potential.

Chapter 10. Debt Management: Minimizing Liabilities, Maximizing Financial Health

Understanding and mastering the concept of debt management is a vital component in a successful wealth creation journey. No financial success story is complete without the stage where one effectively handles their liabilities leading to an optimized financial health.

10.1. Importance of Debt Management

Let's begin by understanding why debt management is crucial. The financial industry often views debt as a tool, a necessary evil, or a stepping stone towards your monetary dreams. If you manage it well, it can be a catalyst towards your business' growth and personal wealth, but if neglected or poorly handled, it can quickly become a debilitating burden, halting your progress and devouring hard-earned income.

The primary goal of debt management is to reduce the cost of that debt. Through various techniques and strategies, we can diminish the high interest rates that erode your income, optimize your repayment schedule, and reduce your overall liability.

10.2. The Debt Cycle

Next, familiarize yourself with the dreaded debt cycle—a perpetual state of mounting debt that seems to grow no matter how aggressively you pay it off. It often starts with a small, manageable debt, but due to poor management and spiraling interest, transforms into a monstrous financial vacuum.

Breaking free from this cycle requires stringent budgeting, disciplined payment of debt, and careful financial planning. It's not only about paying off what you owe but also reforming the financial habits that landed you in debt. Remember: the ultimate aim is not to eliminate debt, but to gain control over it.

10.3. Debt Management Strategies

Now that we've understood why debt management is crucial for your financial health let's delve into some key strategies that can help transform the way you handle your liabilities.

1. Devising a Detailed Budget: A detailed budget listing your income sources and expenditures is the first step towards effective debt management. It helps pinpoint unnecessary spending and areas where you can economize.

2. Prioritizing your Debts: Also known as the 'Avalanche Method,' here, you rank your debts, starting from the highest interest rate. You focus most of your resources on the highest-ranking debt while making minimum payments on the others. Once the first debt is paid off, you move on to the next.

3. Negotiating Interest Rates: Often overlooked, this strategy involves contacting your creditors and negotiating a lower interest rate. Establish a good repayment history and use it as leverage during your negotiation.

4. Debt Consolidation: This involves combining all your debts into a single debt, usually with a lower overall interest rate. It makes management easier, reduces financial stress, and can speed up the debt payment process.

10.4. Managing Credit Card Debt

Credit card debt is a widespread issue influencing financial health worldwide due to high-interest rates and easily available credit. It's a debt that needs particular attention because of its propensity to spiral out of control rapidly.

If you're entrenched in credit card debt, consider transferring your balance to a card with a lower interest rate. However, make sure to read through the terms and conditions thoroughly. A lower introductory rate may soon give way to a much higher one. Also, pay more than the minimum payment each month to decrease your balance faster and reduce the amount of interest accrued.

10.5. Emergency Funds: The Safety Net

Emergencies strike without warning. Unforeseen events like a sudden job loss, a medical emergency, or a necessary home repair can quickly drive you into steep debt if you're unprepared. This is where an emergency fund – a safety net in times of crisis – comes in.

Financial advisors generally recommend saving at least three to six months' worth of living expenses for emergency use. It safeguards you against unforeseen circumstances, reducing dependency on credit. Though building up your emergency fund might detract from paying off your debt temporarily, it offers long-term stability and secures your financial health.

10.6. The Impact of Debt on Investments

Debt and investments are two sides of the same coin - your financial life. Depending on the interest rate and term of your debt, it can even make more financial sense to prioritize investing before hurrying to pay it down. If your debt has a low interest rate, the potential returns from investing in a high-yield account might justify slow repayment.

However, carrying high-interest debt, such as credit card debt, cripples your ability to amass wealth. The gains realized from investments are likely much lower than the cost of maintaining this type of debt. Therefore, managing debt enables you to seamlessly pave your journey towards successful investing, by providing the necessary monetary cushion and financial stability.

Proper debt management isn't just about clambering out of the financial pit you're in; it's about taking control of your opportunities to go from surviving to thriving. Get on top of your debt, and you're one step closer to winning the money game.

Chapter 11. Continuous Learning: Staying Ahead in the Money Game

The world of finance is vast and swiftly evolving, with new concepts, strategies, and asset classes emerging all the time. Embarking on a journey of wealth creation mandates lifelong learning. It's not just about grasping the basic principles of personal finance but also about staying updated with new developments in the global financial ecosystem.

11.1. The Importance of Continuous Learning

Learning about financial management is not a task to be checked off the list but an ongoing process. The financial markets are always in flux, reflecting changes in government policies, corporate performance, and macroeconomic trends. This means that making informed decisions requires keeping abreast of the latest financial news, asset price movements, and forecasts.

It's crucial to educate yourself about different investment classes, such as equities, bonds, mutual funds, real estate, and newer options like cryptocurrencies. Understand how to evaluate each investment opportunity, the pros and cons associated with them, and the level of risk they come with.

11.2. Creating a Learning Plan

A systematic learning plan can make it easier for you to grasp and retain complex financial concepts. Start by identifying your financial goals and researching topics related to them. Choose reliable sources of information, like financial newspapers, investment blogs, and educational websites. Set a regular schedule for this study, even if it's just a few minutes each day.

Remember, your financial learning journey is personal. It should be tailored to your unique circumstances, interests, and goals. Don't fear to delve into areas that might seem complex initially. Small, consistent increments of learning can lead to significant understanding over time.

11.3. Learning through Real-World Application

As the saying goes, 'experience is the best teacher'. Once you have a basic grasp of financial concepts, the best way to forge ahead is to apply the learning in real life. Start by revisiting your personal finances. Re-evaluate your budget, assess your investments, and consider where changes or improvements can be made. With practice and careful risk management, your confidence in your wealth creation prowess should grow.

11.4. Going Beyond Books: Podcasts, Webinars, and Online Courses

In the digital era, there are numerous learning resources at our fingertips, each catering to different learning styles. We can consume information in multimedia formats like podcasts, videos, webinars, and online courses. For finance, numerous free and paid platforms offer courses varying from beginner to advanced levels.

Podcasts and webinars are a great compliment to traditional learning materials. They often feature industry experts offering opinions, analyses, and insights that can help shape your financial strategies.

Integrate these sources into your learning plan to widen your understanding and perspective.

11.5. Building a Financial Network

One of the overlooked approaches to learning is networking. Connecting with financially savvy individuals can provide a wealth of firsthand insights, tips, and strategies. Consider joining financial forums, chat groups, or local clubs where investors meet and discuss their strategies and share their experiences.

11.6. Cultivating Emotional Intelligence

The money game is not just about number-crunching and portfolio strategy - it's also greatly about managing emotions and exercising discipline. Building wealth requires us to make rational financial decisions and avoid impulsive behavior, especially in volatile markets. Emotional intelligence helps us to be mindful of our financial habits and the emotional triggers that can lead to poor decisions.

11.7. Conclusion: Embrace the Journey

Just as in any other game, winning the money game is about mindset as much as it is about skills. See your journey of continuous learning as an integral part of your life - an exploration that empowers you to take ownership of your financial future. Remember that there's no final destination in learning. It's an ongoing process, and the more dedicated you are, the closer you get to winning the money game.

This wraps up our chapter on Continuous Learning. The journey ahead is bound to be exciting, challenging, a little nerve-wracking, perhaps, but ultimately rewarding. Remember, the aim is not to become a financial guru overnight but to gradually improve your financial literacy, take calculated risks, and make informed decisions. After all, wealth creation is not a sprint; it's a marathon.